Write Before Coffee

How to Write Your Book When
You Think You're Not a Writer

By Carlene Hill Byron

Write Before Coffee

Carlene Hill Byron

2024 © by Carlene Hill Byron

All rights reserved. Published 2024.

Printed in the United States of America

Spirit Media and our logos are trademarks of Spirit Media

SpiritMedia.US

www.spiritmedia.us
8045 Arco Corporate Dr STE 130
Raleigh, NC 27617
Books > Reference > Writing, Research & Publishing Guides > Writing > Writing Skills

ebook ISBN: 979-8-89307-032-3

Paperback ISBN: 979-8-89307-033-0

Audiobook ISBN: 979-8-89307-034-7

Library of Congress Control Number: 2024903555

Author's
Introduction

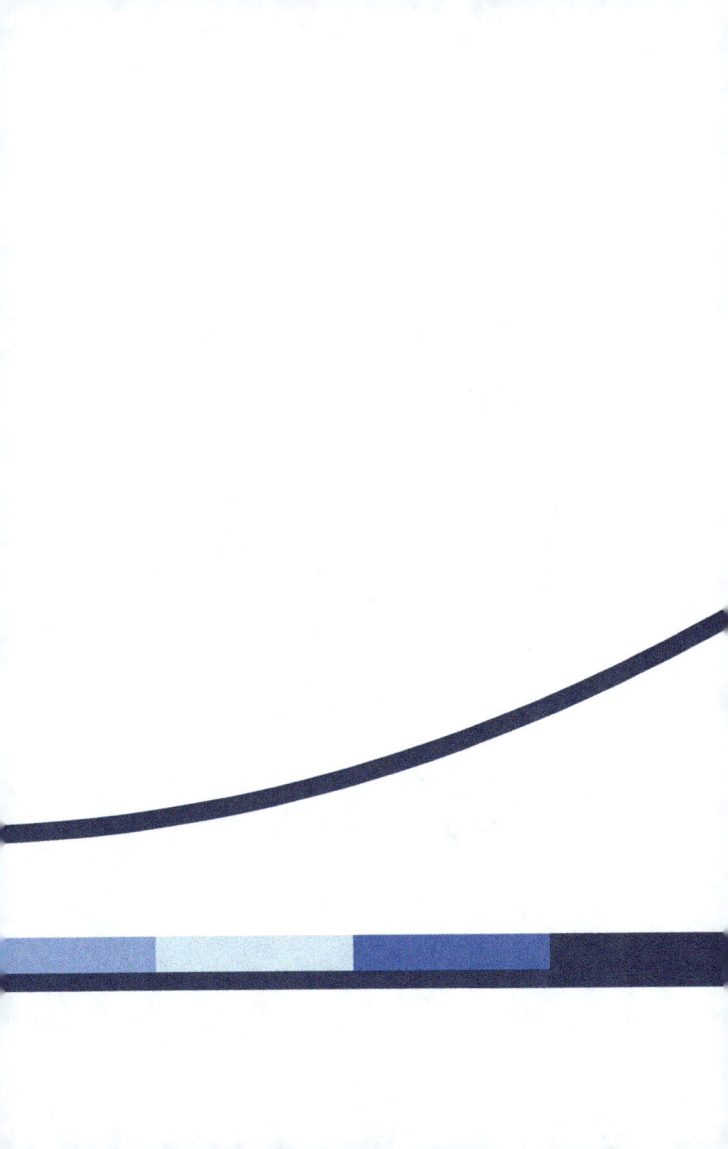

**Carlene
Hill Byron**

Author

Author's Introduction

I came to writing as a career pretty early. I got my first paycheck for an article before I finished college, and I was hooked! At this point, I've worked more than 40 years as a professional writer and editor across a wide range of organizations and disciplines—a daily newspaper, a tech startup, a large engineering company, two regional faith-based nonprofits, a company that supported SEO for an online global marketplace, and a regional disability nonprofit. Today, I'm one of the editors and Angel Writers in Spirit Media.

For me, learning about and writing about so many different things has been fun. But I have always brought to my career the same question which you may also have:

Why write?

Why do people write?

Most fundamentally:

We write to build bridges.

Bridges come in all kinds of styles and capacities. I live in Maine, where people still use bridges that were built more than a century ago. One wire bridge, up in our mountains, has a wooden plank roadbed that's just one lane wide. Some of today's SUVs are too heavy to cross it.

When we write,
we build bridges
with our stories.

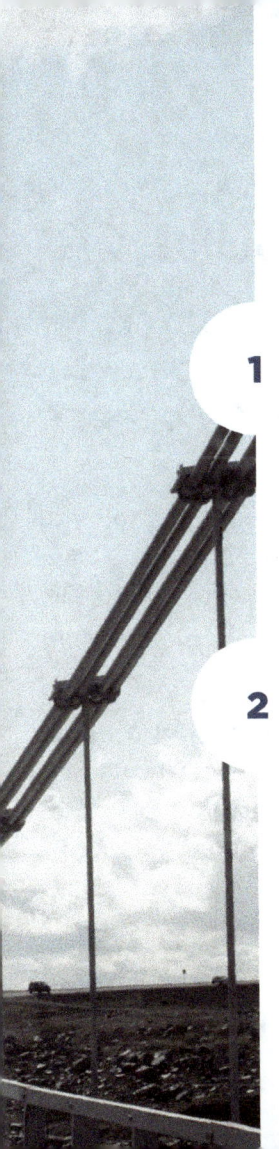

1 **We build bridges between people:** The people whose stories are told and the people who tell them.

2 **We build bridges between people and God:** Because we choose to tell inspiring stories about how God has changed people's lives.

5

What bridge has God prepared you to build?

How can your story carry others closer to God and each other?

We urge our potential authors to listen to God to understand the message He wants to share through them to all of God's people, the people God has called from all the world's 195 nations to know His voice and carry His Word.

You are probably holding this booklet because you are at least beginning to know inside you what message God wants you to carry forward. You might even be experienced at putting your words together in sermons, devotionals, conference talks, blog posts, or more.

What story has God put in you?

What experiences
can you share?

What lessons have
you learned?

How will your
story benefit God's
people?

Fabulous stories from God's people that I've been privileged to help share include:

- Jeremy Kluth's message about learning to memorize God's word.

- Joeth Strickland's stories about God's work to bring essential goods to Christian missions in 105 countries.

- Nora Fozard's flow of biblical wisdom for counseling.

- Richard Convery's novels based among the homeless in Newcastle, New South Wales.

What's the point of writing your story?

God tells us that each one of us is saved by faith—not works—and that God recreates us through Christ into His own masterpiece (work of art), designed to do good works that He's already prepared for us to walk into (Eph. 2:8-10). The stories we have been given to tell encourage and uplift others who need to know the truths we've learned:

- God is with you.

- God is working in and through you.

- God isn't finished with you yet!

Let me tell you the story of just one of our authors. Joeth Strickland started collecting things missionaries needed and shipping them overseas about 40 years ago. Back then, she had her Sunday School class and other friends fill up a few boxes, which she kept in the breezeway of her home until she would ship them. Today, she's running a 17,000-square-foot warehouse and has shipped to Christian non-governmental organizations in 105 nations so far. That includes 42 full 40-foot containers to Ukraine in the first 21 months of the war.

Is God finished with Joeth yet? I don't think so! And God's work in the world is being accomplished because of her and other faithful Christians like her who know that God isn't finished with them yet.

How do you **find the words** to tell your story in a book?

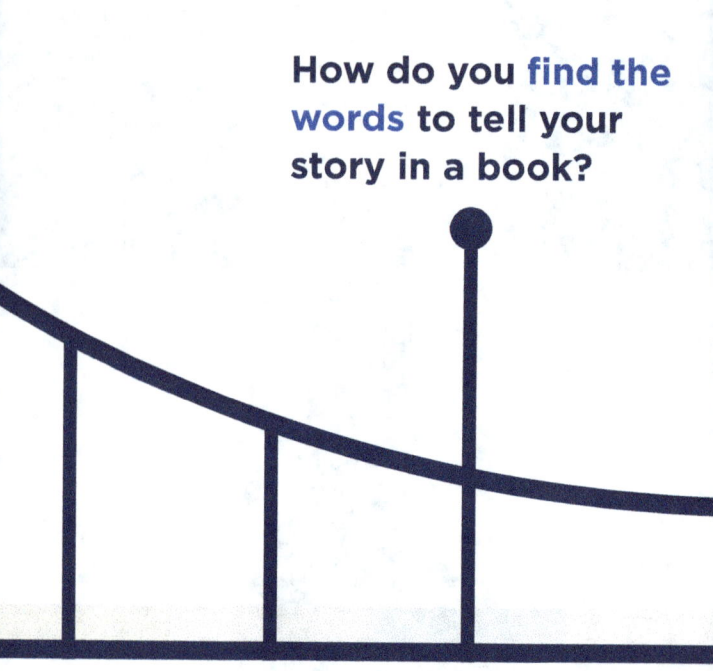

You may be an experienced wordsmith… BUT a book is a different thing. So we'll talk more about that soon.

Where do you find words for a book? You can collect them from things that you and other people have already written, and you can create them fresh.

Words you've already written

Many of us create text regularly for specific uses:

Blogs

Sermons

Opinion Pieces

Speeches

These can become part of your book project.

Words you find and save

Many of us are always finding great quotes and ideas in our regular media diet:

Streaming media you follow

News media you follow

Books you're reading

Stories you stream

You'll find your own favorite way to save words you've found. Some people like to use:

1. Bins or folders by subtopic

2. An online tool like OneNote or Scrivener

3. Journal books

4. 3x5 cards in your purse or pocket

5. Notes: I love the little sticky tabs I can put into a book I'm reading when I find something I need to make a note of later.

Words you create for this project

Creating text can feel challenging. That empty page seems SO intimidating! Here are two secrets from a long-time professional writer:

- Pro Writer Secret #1: If you're not a Pro Writer, of course that blank page is intimidating! Would you step onto a Broadway stage and start dancing without feeling intimidated?

- Pro Writer Secret #2: Even those of us who write every single day can get stuck at the beginning of a project … a chapter … an outline.

So we'll talk later about some tricks
for starting to fill that blank page.

How do you START writing a book?

There are **two basic strategies** for writing a book, and successful writers use either or even sometimes both:

1 **Establish an outline and write to it.** This is how Spirit Media CEO Kevin White has written five books so far.

2 **Write until you discover the outline.** This is how I, as a Spirit Media Angel Writer, wrote my own first book and have worked with Spirit Media clients to write five books in 16 months.

For writers who have not written a book before, having this kind of range among the people supporting you is helpful. If you're working with one of our Angel Writers at Spirit Media, we'll help you plan, organize, and complete your book—typically in just three months!

First, we'll talk with you about your vision and plans for the book. Is it a book you'll use to teach others? A memoir that will encourage its readers? A tool to help memorably brand your business or ministry? What do you hope this book will accomplish?

Next we'll talk through any ideas you already have for what should be in this book. You may have a full outline or you might just have some bullet points in a notebook. You might have a huge pile of content you've written as sermons or blog posts that need to be reorganized to fit the format of a book. In any of these situations, an Angel Writer can help you structure your book so it's easy for your readers to follow and enjoy.

An Angel Writer can also help you expand your initial ideas into larger sections of text. Many people like to have their Angel Writer interview them and then draft text from their conversations. Others like to send their own text drafts to the Angel Writer for refinement. Either way, your Angel Writer will be checking back with you regularly to confirm that the text being drafted sounds like you and is telling your story the way you want it told.

Your Angel Writer will recommend attention-grabbing chapter heads and subheads as your work through your book project. These make it easier for your readers to continue being drawn through your message in a time when people find it difficult to sustain focus.

According to your preference, you will review your book either as a full draft or one section at a time. Most authors meet just one hour a week with their Angel Writer and are surprised how easy and fast it is to complete the book that's been on your mind for ages—a book you will be proud of.

The busy founder of an all-volunteer organization serving Christian missions across the world, Joeth Strickland wanted to explain the how and why of Crossing All Borders Ministry in a way that new volunteers and potential donors would understand. Her book, Faithful in Small Things: How God Grew a Ministry from One Home to Serve 104 Nations, was written in three months and published the same year. Joeth signed on immediately for a second book, focusing on how US Christians were supporting people in the war zone in Ukraine.

If you're like Joeth—way too busy to write— an Angel Writer can make it simple for you to finally finish your book.

Every **personality** has its own favorite way of writing, and all of these ways to write are effective. Since your personality is a gift to you from God, you can trust that God can gift you with words according to the way your personality works.

How does your personality prefer to write?

 **Visual processor -** You learn by seeing things. As a writer, you may prefer to put your ideas on a screen, on a wall, or somewhere where you can look at them.

 **Auditory processor -** You learn by hearing things. As a writer, you may want to talk through your ideas with others, dictate them on your phone, or into a dictation software.

 **Tactile processor -** You learn by touching and moving things around. As a writer, you may want to handwrite your texts on paper, and even physically cut and paste the pages.

How does your writing experience affect your writing today?

The writing experience you have will also shape your way of writing. So once upon a time, I wrote a 600-word monthly column for a Christian newspaper. That got me in the habit of writing and thinking in 600-word bursts. To this day, I start with 600-word text sections under the various headings and subheadings, then expand sections from there.

A person who often prepares sermons and speeches is used to thinking in blocks of words that take 20-40 minutes to read aloud. That means they will tend to create text in units of 2,500-4,500 words, or 10-20 manuscript pages.

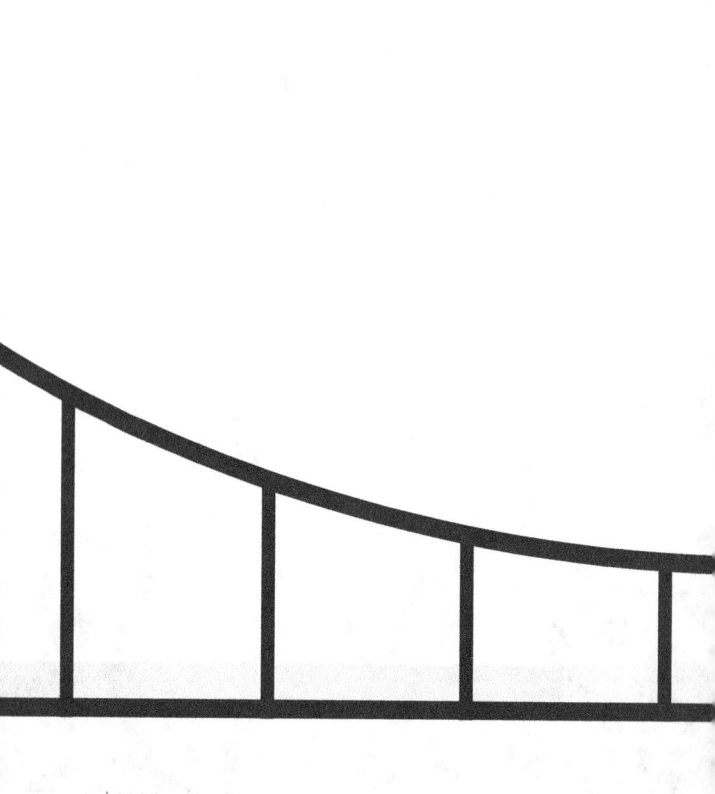

4 Pro Tips if you have a message AND you're not used to writing:

Getting started can be difficult. Writer's block happens even to those who write every day. The blank page can be intimidating. So here are 4 Pro Tips for getting started.

1
Write.

If you're not a professional writer, you're not expected to be highly skilled in writing. That's why you get an editor involved. The purpose of writing is to write, not to produce the finished text today. So just start dumping words on your screen, in your notebook, or on your 3x5 cards. Just write!

2 Write whenever and wherever.

Until writing is comfortable for you, experiment with the times and places and tools. Do you like to draft your text with a pen in a notebook sitting in a comfy chair? On your laptop looking out from your screen porch? Do you focus better when it's busy around you or when you have absolute quiet? Are you more able to think about your chosen audience of readers when you are somewhere they hang out—your veterans center, a particular coffee shop, the Sunday school classroom? Experimenting with where and when you write may help you find your own best place and way to write.

3 Write. Don't edit!

Writing and editing are two different ways of working on text, and they use two different parts of the brain. If you try to edit as you go, you'll get caught up in polishing the first sentences for days on end. Trust me, this is the voice of experience speaking!

Writing creates a small mountain of content from which you are going to mine the right words in the process of editing. But if you don't write first, you won't have a mountain to mine.

Finally, here is the **WEIRDEST TIP** you'll ever hear about how to write ...

4 Write before you wake up.

Now, I'm not an early bird so believe me, I'm not pushing that "successful people start their day at 4 a.m." idea. Nor am I suggesting that you should count on God to give you your text in a dream (although if you often wake up with ideas for your book, it can help to have a notebook next to your bed).

What I'm offering you now is just a trick you can play on your brain to make it work best for you as a writer.

The part of your brain that creates–the writing part–actually "wakes up" earlier than the part of your brain that edits. If you give yourself a few weeks of early morning writing, you'll learn what it feels like to create without having an internal editor yelling at you about your spelling and where the commas belong. What has worked for me is to get up at least 30 minutes earlier than I'm used to and go straight to my desk. NO COFFEE. The editor loves coffee!

After you do this for a few weeks, you'll know what it feels like to write without an interrupting editor, and you'll be able to do this trick whenever you want.

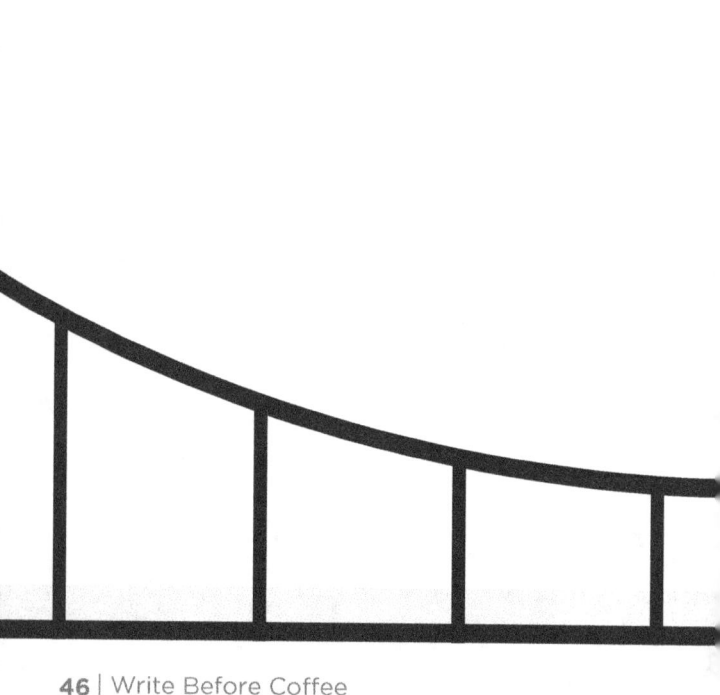

An example: How I organize my own book writing

Everyone organizes their writing projects in ways that work for them. I'm a tactile learner first, a visual learner second. So I did the working organization for my first book with sticky notes. For me, sticky notes free me to shift elements as my thinking changes, and to see how the different parts relate to each other. For this book I used:

- **Green for chapter heads**
- **Pink for chapter subdivisions**
- **Yellow for key scriptures**
- **Blue for applications**

49

If you work with one of our writers, the way we organize your project will vary depending on who you work with and what seems to work best for you.

- This is why it helps to bring a professional writer and editor into the project.

- You bring the inspiration.

- We bring the experience and skill that build your bridge effectively to your readers.

What's the shape of the story you're telling?

Part of organizing a story is discovering its shape. Is this a story that moves straight to a goal, or one that involves a lot of being knocked down and getting back up?

There are a great many different story designs that are commonly used in the 21st century. One of my favorites is something called The Hero's Journey, which often applies to stories from Christian living:

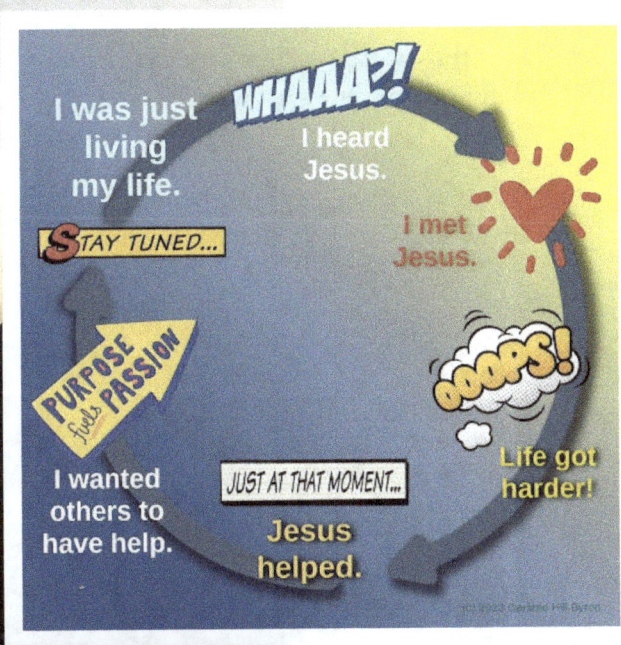

Here's how this story structure works. It starts at the top left and continues around the circle:

- "I was just living my life …" Seems kind of boring, right? But in this story structure, this is where we start: Where we are, doing whatever it is that we do.

- Then the hero hears the voice of a mentor … in our stories, this is often the voice of Jesus.

- The hero meets the mentor, Jesus, and is enamored of His grace, wisdom, and expertise. Surely this is the beginning of a fabulous life where everything is perfect!

- But no! Life actually gets harder!!

- And just at that moment, the mentor–Jesus–helps.

- Our hero is so grateful that she or he wants others to have that same help from that same wonderful mentor. So …

- Fueled with new purpose and passion, she or he returns home.

- Stay tuned for what will happen next!

Most of our authors have grown through many challenges, and this structure allows the story to continue beyond the first success, or even the first book.

If you're uncertain how to shape your story, it's helpful to work with our team, because we're experienced at this.

How Story Partners Can Help

Spirit Media can connect you with a wide range of story partners who are able to help you develop your story from concept to publication to global sales.

We help you develop your text.

Project planning: to work through what you want to say and how it might be organized. You set the goal, we can help you break it into pieces and keep track of status so you can get it done. Jeremy Kluth had a hard deadline to have his book in hand for a conference, and we worked with him to meet his goal.

Accountability: to your desired schedule. When you sign a contract with us, you set your target date for completion and we help you attain your goal.

Skilled writers and editors: to help you tell your story effectively and with excellence. We all have written things in school. But most of us haven't written a book. It helps to work with someone who's been there. Your expertise is in your subject area, whether that's an area of ministry or your life experience. Writers and editors have developed expertise in communicating through words.

We help you build bridges beyond the book.

1 **Engaging the Amazon beast.** It is a beast, and it's a shape-shifter. We're always learning how to deal with Amazon's latest so you can focus on your own mission.

2 **Translation for a global market.** To date, we've published in English, Hindi, Telugu, and more. We also just brought Spanish translators on board. If your ideas need to reach the world, no publisher is more on board with your goals than Spirit Media.

3 **Book design and branding.** We design books so they are both appealing in the reader's hands and appealing as a thumbnail on Amazon, where the largest number of potential readers will see them first.

4 **Media releases.** There's a specific skill to getting your story out to interested media around the world. We can do this for you.

5 **Digital marketing (SEO text).** I call this the poetry of the machine. If you ever wrote traditional poetry, you remember choosing words so they fit a particular rhythm and rhyme scheme. SEO text is likewise a specific writing style designed so search engines will find your book, your blog, your website, your promotional content.

What Kind of Bridge Are You Building with Your Words?

- We've talked about your purpose in writing: The message God has given you that burns in your heart and must be communicated to others.

- We've talked about bridging: The bridge that your written words provide between you and the people you want to touch.

- We've talked about the process of writing: Capturing your words, editing your words, and working with Spirit Media to build a strong and successful bridge between what God has given you and the people around the world who need to read it.

Building a quality bridge is important.

- Some bridges just aren't designed for people to cross!

- Some bridges are really hard—even hazardous—to cross!

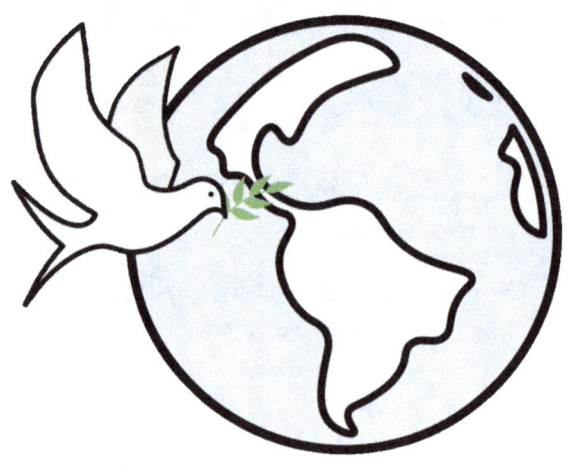

At Spirit Media:

We write to build bridges for the
NATIONS.

We write to build bridges for the
AGES.

We write to build bridges to God's
KINGDOM.

Join us in building the bridges that carry people toward living God's work in God's world.

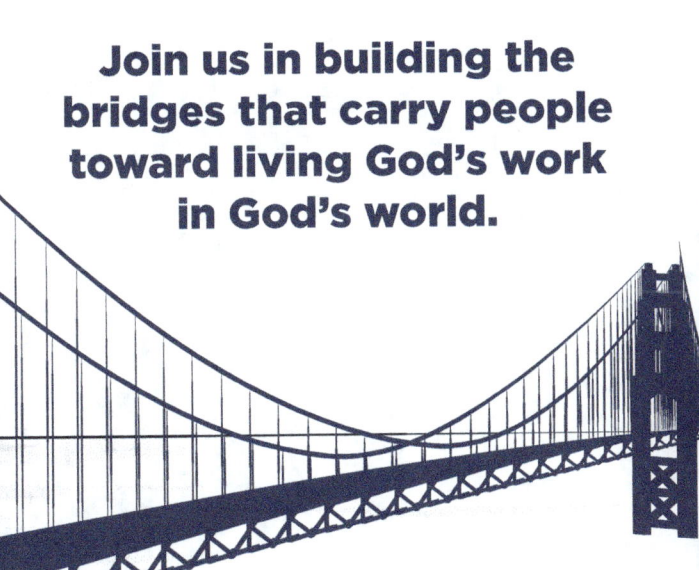

HOW CAN THE CHURCH SUPPORT OUR OWN PEOPLE **STRUGGLING WITH MENTAL HEALTH?**

"Full of wisdom."

BARBARA HEMPHILL
Founder, Productive
Environment Institute

"Wise, poignant, and immensely practical."

WARREN KINGHORN, MD, ThD
Duke University
Medical Center and Duke
Divinity School

"Very welcome and deeply encouraging."

JOHN R. PETEET, MD
Harvard Medical School

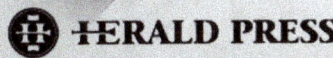

HeraldPress.com • 1-800-245-7894

Reality ministries

Creating opportunities for adults with and without developmental disabilities to experience belonging, kinship and the life-changing Reality of Christ's love in Durham, NC.

Interested in learning more?

🌐 realityministries.org

✉️ info@realityministries.org

📷 @realitydurhamchapelhill

DISCOVER HOW WE'VE HELPED OTHERS

PUBLISHING

BRANDING

MARKETING